Wors in the City

by
John Bentham
Assistant Curate, St. Agnes, Burmantofts, Leeds

GROVE BOOKS LIMITED
Bramcote   Nottingham   NG9 3DS

CONTENTS

	Page
1. Introduction....................................	3
2. Some Aspects of the Urban Culture.................	4
(a) Urban Priority Areas	
(b) The Working Classes	
(c) The Church and the Working Classes	
(d) Communication in Working-Class Cultures	
3. Worship and Life................................	8
4. Some Principles for Worship in UPAs...............	10
(a) Relaxing the Structures	
(b) Small is Beautiful	
(c) Promoting the Visual	
(d) Bringing in Life	
(e) Making Music	
(f) Learning about Silence	
5. Summary—Lessons for the Wider Church.............	23
Appendix 1: Select Bibliography.....................	23
Appendix 2: The section on Worship (6.99-6.113) in *Faith in the City*..	24

ACKNOWLEDGEMENTS

Early impetus to my line of enquiry was given by a seminar on the 'Spirituality of the City' at the *Greenbelt* Festival in 1983, so thanks to Neville Black for that and subsequent comments. I'm grateful to Colin Buchanan and other staff at St. John's College Nottingham who kept me at it, and to the clergy in various UPA parishes on Merseyside for help with the original research. The last phase of the booklet's development owes much to the space and inspiration given to me by my vicar, Chris Burch, and the life and worship of the people of St. Agnes' Burmantofts. Not forgetting various typists, especially my sister Janet, and all those who read early drafts and commented on them. If I had a spare page to dedicate it to somebody it would say 'To the memory of Susie Whiting'.

QUOTATIONS FROM *FAITH IN THE CITY*

are reproduced by kind permission of Church House Publishing

THE COVER PICTURE

... is by Steve Pickering

First Impression April 1986

ISSN 0144—1728

ISBN 1 85174 024 4

1. INTRODUCTION

The task of our churches in Urban Priority Areas is an immense one, and has been expertly summed up in *Faith in the City*.[1] There are implications for all areas of our church life, although the Commission actually had little to say about worship. Further work is necessary, especially since it appears that those churches which are growing in such areas are very often characterized by lively and attractive worship. Yet the observations which the Commission does make with regard to worship are perceptive, and bear out the experience of many Christians ministering in Urban Priority Areas with whom I have spoken. The section on worship is printed as as Appendix to this booklet. In one respect, talking about the externals of Sunday worship is not a radical enough step. The lack of indigenous leadership would seem to be a more pressing question. Yet the two are inter-related, and worship is one sphere of ministry in which that leadership must be sought and encouraged.

Should worship in the city be any different from worship elsewhere? The answer to that question hinges on your definition of worship, but as I trace what I believe to be the inter-relationship of worship and everyday life I hope that it will become clear that I believe the answer to that question to be 'yes'. Worship is not restricted to some personal spiritual world, nor does it involve disengagement from the society in which we live. The joys and sorrows of life in our Urban Priority Areas—and indeed of whichever community we live in—must feed in to our services of worship.

This booklet is limited to some extent by space and by my own experience, in that it concentrates mostly on what is developing in worship in predominantly white working-class communities, and not specifically on multi-ethnic communities. However, since the aim is to suggest principles and not to prescribe action, it will hopefully provide discussion material for all Urban Priority Area churches. Indeed, so clergy-dominated is our worship throughout the country that many different sorts of churches may find it provokes thought.

A brief portrait is painted of Urban Priority Areas, and the distinctive features of communication in working-class culture are examined. A definition of worship is developed, especially in its relationship to life and culture. The sociology and the theology is then used to ask hard questions of our current worship practices. Some principles for worship in Urban Priority Areas are suggested, and some examples cited—some things which have only been tried once or twice, some gleaned from my own and other ministers' experience. The discussion and exploration will need to go on, and I would be delighted to receive comments, and to hear of both successes and failures in similar experiments.

---

[1] The Report of the Archbishop of Canterbury's Commission on Urban Priority Areas (Church House Publishing, 1985).

2. SOME ASPECTS OF URBAN CULTURE

(a) Urban Priority Areas

The term 'Urban Priority Area' (UPA) has come to be used of districts in our cities which are of specially disadvantaged character. They are places which suffer from economic decline, physical decay and social disintegration. The typical UPA is an old port or manufacturing area connected to an outmoded staple industrial process. It may be at the centre of a conurbation like Hackney, or it may be spatially displaced from the inner city as a corporation estate on the outskirts, like Kirby to the east of Liverpool, or Killingworth outside Newcastle. But whatever it unique features, it will exhibit three kinds of blight—economic, physical and social—which are essential to the definition. Such is the UPA, constituting a different Britain, whose people are prevented from entering fully into the mainstream of the normal life of the nation.[1] This booklet is not the place to describe or analyze the social factors of UPAs in any further depth—we now have a superb resource in *Faith in the City*. Suffice it to say that it is a complex story of mismatch between people, skills, housing and jobs which planning has failed to overcome, and we now have whole communities where feelings of powerlessness and lack of self-confidence have developed.

> 'UPAs shelter disproportionate numbers of vulnerable people—the unemployed, the unskilled, the uneducated, the sick, the old, and the disadvantaged minority ethnic groups. They are places which suffer conspicuously from low income, dependence on state bureaucracies and social security, ill health, crime, family breakdown and homelessness.'[2]

The picture is a grim one, and sadly the church in such areas is largely seen as irrelevant.[3] Congregations are mostly small and declining. The problem can be traced back to the Industrial Revolution, and the failure of the church to come to grips with the burgeoning cities. Whilst it is clear that many of our inner city areas are now very mixed multi-racial communities, it is instructive to look at the historical root of the problem—the church's alienation from the working classes.

(b) The Working Classes

There is not one universally-accepted criterion for distinguishing between classes. Some definitions have been made in terms of occupation, some in terms of income. Yet changes in employment patterns, and the increasing affluence and mobility of many traditionally working-class people, have rendered these criteria suspect. The gulf between the classes is certainly not as great as it once might have been. Yet many sociologists would argue that the norms, values and attitudes of the working and middle classes still differ to some degree. By making what appear to be gross generalizations, we can hopefully identify differences between the subcultures which have implications for the church and its worship and mission. The plural 'classes' will be used to acknowledge the looseness of the classification. No condescension whatever is intended in the use the phrase 'working class'. There is no question of one class being *superior* to another, simply *different.*

---

[1] *Faith in the City* section 1:17.
[2] *Faith in the City* section 1:23.
[3] *Faith in the City* section 2:3.

SOME ASPECTS OF URBAN CULTURE

Traditionally, working-class people lived in close-knit communities associated with long-established industries. They were generally manual workers, in a trade rather than a profession. Most of those in work would receive a weekly wage rather than a monthly salary. Examples of the main industries served in would be coal mining, electricity supply, shipbuilding, the steel industry, building, road haulage, the motor industry, and public transport. This group has been hit hardest by the spiralling unemployment of the late 1970's and early 1980's, and thus definition by reference to jobs alone is now becoming even less sufficient.

The *group* is a common feature of working-class culture. Home life is based on the family unit and often the extended family. Tight working communities are a thing of the past in many places, yet you only have to consider the solidarity of the 1984/5 miners' strike to know that they still exist. The tightly packed terraced housing of industrial cities has also largely disappeared, but a great spirit of solidarity still persists. This has its roots in the need of the manual worker to improve his situation by collective action. In contrast, middle-class culture places an emphasis on individual achievement and success is seen in terms of individual effort.

Common external circumstances (such as housing and employment) tend to produce common inward attitudes and patterns of thought.[1] Working-class attitudes (for example, to work, government, marriage, religion) have not been as fast to change along with occupational and social upheaval as we might expect. Sociologists of the 1950s and 1960s proposed theories of embourgeoisement, whereby increasing numbers of manual workers were becoming more prosperous, and supposedly more middle-class, as they moved to newer suburbs. In one respect this was found to be true, in that the worker often became more privatized and family-centred, rather than community-centred. Yet it was not found that other middle-class norms and values were adopted. There has undeniably been *some* degree of assimilation between the classes, and the discussion of its degree will no doubt continue. But the distinctions between the classes have not totally disappeared and a truly working-class Christianity has not really emerged in any strength in England.

(c) The Church and the Working Classes

'The Church of England's most enduring problem of the city has been its relationship with the urban working class'[2]

A careful study of history shows that the Church in this country has not attracted the working-classes in significant numbers since the Industrial Revolution. The nature of church-going *prior* to this period is the subject of another debate, yet it seems that the movement of large numbers of the rural population to the towns with the onset of industrialization disturbed patterns of church-going. Increasingly, many of the working-classes in the cities had never been to church. The rapidly growing cities were a problem as a whole for the established Church, yet this was clearest in the working-class districts. The churches were seen as being on the side of the establishment, and most were middle-class and remote.[3]

---

[1] See the important work of Hoggart *The Uses of Literacy* (Pelican, 1958) for comparison of middle-class and working-class thoughts and attitudes.

[2] *Faith in the City* section 2:7.

[3] *Faith in the City* sections 2:5 to 2:20 analyzes some possible reasons for this failure.

During the late nineteenth century a large number of small Christian initiatives, often expressing some form of social concern, sprang up in attempts to bridge the gap. There were Missions, Settlements, Labour Churches, Ragged Schools and the 'Pleasant Sunday Afternoons', to name but a few. Within the Anglican Church both evangelicals and anglo-catholics were responsible for some flourishing parishes—often as a result of large programmes of mid-week activities, and teams of lay volunteers. The Salvation Army and the similar Anglican initiative, the Church Army, also began at this time in response to the same need. Yet often these initiatives were concerned primarily with the moral and spiritual state of city areas, showing little acknowledgement of the deep-seated economic and social problems. A rather paternalistic attitude sometimes developed, simply serving to perpetuate the sense of alienation of the working classes.

Unfortunately the 'success' stories were isolated and, if we use church attendance as at least an indicator, then the proportion of worshippers in working-class districts was extremely small when compared with middle-class districts. Some Baptist and Anglican churches were attracting congregations numbering in their hundreds, but many more thousands of people stayed away. Many would not have thought of themselves as less religious, but would not have expressed their religion in terms of attending church regularly. Neither is there a lack of religious feeling in many working-class people today. Our task is to show them the God who is already in their midst. Are we talking the right language?

(d) Communication in Working-Class Cultures

A classic study of life in a Yorkshire mining community, observes:
> 'In conversation about work and football, general considerations or abstractions hardly ever appear. The discussion is almost always about concrete cases, whether of actual incidents at the colliery, or actual incidents on the field of play. There is a scarcity of conversation on the level of general principles. Any attempt to do so is dismissed as "talk"—that is, empty argument. Credit goes to the man who knows a lot of concrete details.'[1]

This concreteness is a well-documented feature of working-class language, and has important implications for our discussion of worship. The conversation of the working-class life is more about the intimate, the sensory, the detailed, and the personal. Hoggart[2] suggested that interest is focussed on local day-to-day experience, rather than wider issues, philosophies or world-views. This is not to be seen as a *lower* order of communication, but a different use of words. For words perform entirely different functions within different social settings. The form and use of language within the working classes seems to represent a totally different way of responding to, and appropriating, experience.

The rather eccentric work of Marshall McLuhan supports this thesis from a different angle.[3] He highlighted the growing preference for a life of sensation rather than of thoughts. His analysis of electronic technology and the media suggested that print encouraged perception of the world in visual, spatial terms—uniform, connected and continuous—a linear series. This

---

[1] Denis, Henriques and Slaughter *Coal is our Life* (Eyre and Spottiswood, 1956).
[2] *Op. cit.* Also see Benington *Culture, Class and Christian Beliefs* (SU, 1973) for examples.
[3] McLuhan and Fiore *The Medium is the Message* (Penguin, 1967).

he termed 'hot' media. In contrast to this ordered sequence of stimuli, McLuhan identified 'cool' media, which consisted of a barrage of sense-impressions. The modern pop video is a development of what he was describing, with its rapid barrage of sounds and images. The preference of working-class young people for music and picture, rather than reading reflects this preference for immediate sensory experience rather than abstract analytical thought (and incidentally for shared *communal* experience rather than isolated *individual* activity). We see why a Christianity that only offers 'beliefs', 'promises' and 'doctrines' mediated by words, fails to provide the sort of sensorial evidence—seen, felt, touched and heard—that many require.[1] Working-class people would be more at ease if our media for communicating Christianity were 'cool' not 'hot'!

The investigation of the content of working-class speech and middle-class speech has allowed us more understanding of this phenomenon. The important work of Bernstein[2] demonstrated that working-class speech prefers description to analysis, and is more sensitive to content than to structure. He found that middle-class speech consisted of complex sentences, made more use of qualfiers, and was more likely to set up subtle relationships between ideas. By contrast, working-class speech consisted of shorter, grammatically simpler, sentences. The active rather than the passive voice was stressed, sentences were linked only by the simplest joining words and often left unfinished. A small stock of standard familiar phrases was referred to. Bernstein's definitions of these two types of speech were labelled 'restricted code' and 'elaborate code' respectively. Restricted code communication does not rely so much on the actual words themselves, and their intrinsic meaning and relationship to one another, but on the rhythm, stress and pitch of the words, and the bodily and facial postures and gestures which accompany them. (Note, for example, how a swear-word can be used in a friendly way or a threatening way). Elaborated code draws on a greater vocabulary to express the same feelings.

The focus of restricted speech code is often only the particular community in which that group of people is set. Regular appeal is made to concrete and specific examples within the community, to 'folk myths' and oral tradition. A lot of language is in terms of the known and the experienced, the real and the actual—much more embodied, less theoretical.

It is further believed that different speech patterns have an effect on people's processes of reasoning. There are therefore implications not only for the language of worship but for the form of the church's preaching and teaching ministries. In general, working-class speech tends to be more inductive—reasoning from particular cases to general conclusions, whilst middle-class forms of speech are more deductive—beginning with premises or accepted principles in order to judge a particular case. Christ's own use of metaphor and parable would therefore ideally suit working-class audiences and their preference for concrete graphic description. His parables disclosed God through simple and familiar day-to-day situations.

With this picture of the general patterns of communication within working-class cultures, we turn to consider worship.

[1] See Benington *Culture, Class and Christian Beliefs* (Scripture Union, 1973).
[2] Basil Berstein *Class, Codes and Control* (Vol. 1) (RKP 1971).

3. WORSHIP AND LIFE

Worship is not true worship if it is divorced from the everyday life of the worshipper and the wider community. Worship services are suspect if they do not allow expression of the lives of the constituent worshippers. The truth of these statements becomes more evident if we are more precise in our definition of 'worship'. Worship, 'worth-ship' is giving God his worth, and God is surely worth out total self-offering. We bring to God everything that we are—our joys and sorrows, our gifts and our failings, our praise and our anger. Furthermore, it is not 'I' on my own who comes, but 'we'—a community. We bring the ups and downs of our shared lives and the events and feelings of the world God created. The honesty of the Psalms is a precedent for us in its praise and in its lament.

Both Jesus and the Old Testament prophets denounced the elaborate paraphernalia of worship when it had become divorced from the everyday lives of the worshippers. If people were praying to a just God, then justice could not be ignored in their business dealings (for example Amos 5.21ff.). If worship of a God of self-giving love was motivated be self-enhancement or reputation, then it was not true worship (Luke 18.9f.). A gift brought to God is welcomed only if the giver is at peace ('shalom') with others (Matthew 5.24). Celebration cannot be divorced from caring and the pursuit of justice.

God takes ordinary things and consecrates them. The incarnation of God in Jesus Christ shows us that God penetrates our ordinary life in order to open the gates of heaven to us. The Christian community is called to represent the *world* before *God:*
> 'identifying with it, agonizing, suffering, giving time and life and possessions for it, weeping and laughing for it, celebrating, dancing and joying for it, offering obedient lives and sacrifices of praise and thanksgiving, bringing it before God in prayer.'[1]

So worship is the moment-by-moment acknowledgement of obedient and loving service to God. When Christians gather to *express* their worship—the worship that is already all of their lives—then there are many elements which should be expressed. There needs to be a freedom for every member to bring of their lives to Sunday worship. Many of our current worship services therefore fall far short of true worship (and not only those in the city). A basic need in most Christian communities is to move away from worship led and dominated by one highly-educated male. He alone cannot express the fulness of God's creation, nor the feelings and experiences of the whole community.

The Christian community is also called to represent *God* before the *world.* Here there is a tension. If the concerns of the world, and the environment in which we live, are allowed to dominate our worship at the expense of a vision of the transcendent God, then we are not given the hope and the peace that will serve to energize our service of the kingdom.

> 'We have to strike that sweet harmony between on the one hand the Jesus in God who shares in the suffering, the evictions, the

---

[1] Jim Punton *God's Radical Alternative* (Frontier Youth Trust) p.7.

earthly ordinariness, and on the other the high Godness of God, who is infinitely distinct from all created things'[1]

African and West Indian churches in this country impart terrific strength to their members in vibrant worship which celebrates the coming kingdom, despite the troubles of their inner-city existence.[2] Hope for a better life removed from our current suffering has to have a place.

Yet in urban culture perhaps it is the immanence of God which needs most emphasis. The urban poor are much more likely to believe that God is infinitely removed from them and all their doings. Yet the transcendent God is to be made real and concrete in the daily lives of his people. As people look at the Christian community they should see acts which transcend this materialistic and selfish world in which we live. In my experience the most attractive worship is only a reflection of the attractive lives of the Christians who are worshipping.

The sense of community, the sense of belonging, is an important aspect of worship. Many Anglican services of the past have appeared to give only a framework for personal and private devotion. This does not figure in the New Testament picture of worship, and is largely a reflection of the middle-classness of much Anglicanism. The worship of the early church seems to have been characterized by spontaneity and contribution by all the members of the body of Christ: 'speaking to one another in psalms, hymns and spiritual songs' (Eph. 5.19; Col. 3.16), each coming with something to give: 'a hymn, or a word of instruction, a revelation, a tongue or an interpretation' (1 Cor. 14.26f.). Many of the services of our established churches are arranged to exclude anything remotely like spontaneity! Lives that are given in the service of the kingdom are shared lives, and so worship must surely be shared worship. Our modern Anglican eucharistic rites have re-emphasized the corporate nature of worship: '. . . one body, because we all share in one bread'; physically demonstrated in the Peace '. . . let us then pursue all that makes for peace and builds up our common life'. Yet this rich community symbolism is not sufficient if left as recited words. There must be room for the real contribution of the varying gifts and different experiences of the individual believers. There should therefore be an unpredictability, a spontaneity about worship. This, then, forces us to ask questions about our liturgy.

---

[1] Jim Thompson *Worship and Housing Estates* (Southwark diocese, Internal Paper).
[2] See John Root *Encountering Westindian Pentecostalism* Grove Booklet on Ministry and Worship No. 66, 1979).

4. SOME PRINCIPLES FOR WORSHIP IN UPAs

We have noted that life in urban working-class culture tends to be informal and spontaneous; that it is more group-based and less individualistic; and that the visual and the story with concrete details is used more to communicate than is the conceptual. We have also noted that God has become remote to many urban people, yet that true worship has its foundations in everyday life. This all suggests that the following principles have an important part to play as we meet to worship our God in the City:

(a) Relaxing the Structures

'There has been a clear plea that the formal liturgies so beloved of the wider church must be complemented in UPAs by more informal and spontaneous acts of worship and witness.'[1]

If local culture is noisy, informal, chaotic, boisterous and strong in feelings, then formal and careful services with nothing 'out of place' can be very alienating. The greater honesty and straightforwardness of working-class culture is in contrast to the stifling of emotions that is deemed respectable by the middle classes. This is plain, for example, in the open emotion of many working-class funerals and weddings. In order to allow this natural spontaneity to break through, planning of worship does not need to be abandoned altogether. In fact, it requires a great deal of care and time to ensure that those taking part feel secure enough to be informal and natural. It can be very unnerving not to have *any* fixed points of reference in the service. There will be barriers of shyness to be overcome with loving care. Some people will have to be quietly asked in private before they read a lesson, pray, or contribute in some other way. For their first few contributions they may have to be helped to prepare—projecting their voices in reading, writing or just reading a simple prayer. The burden of leading five minutes or more of intercessory prayer is too large for a beginner.

Many evangelical churches will consider that a time of open prayer gives everybody adequate chance to contribute in worship. Yet the truth of the matter is that only the able few will pray, in certain rather set ways, and many will be left feeling inadequate. There is a place for simple litanies, or prayers deliberately constructed to encourage short responses from as many people as possible—simply naming those who are sick, or in need of prayer out aloud, or offering one-sentence prayers or thanks to God for what he has done in one's life. Some congregations split into small groups during services in order to pray, or use 'chain' prayer—praying around in a circle in turn, passing on simply by touching the person next to them, remaining silent if they wish to.

Liturgy

Anglicans and other liturgically-minded churches must ask themselves if their liturgy is flexible enough to allow the expression of urban life that has been outlined. There are advantages in using liturgy. It can serve to

---

[1] *Faith in the City* section 6:111.

SOME PRINCIPLES FOR WORSHIP IN UPAs

prevent various innovations and emphases which owe nothing to sound Christian theology from growing up unchecked. Two thousand years of rich heritage in worship cannot be ignored. Liturgy can present us with the fruits of experience and careful doctrine. It offers us a balanced diet which can prevent us from over-emphasizing one or more aspects of our faith at the expense of others. Praise, prayer, thanks, confession, proclamation and other themes are presented in a carefully considered proportion.

There is a security which liturgy brings in its very familiarity. There need to be elements in a service which form a sufficiently familiar pattern for people to be set free from wondering what to do and say next. Even those denominations which boast a freedom in worship eventually settle into fairly set ways of doing things. The use of liturgy acknowledges the value of this, and can *still* provide opportunities for the contribution of the moment. If some liturgy is allowed to become part of us, it can be a real aid to worship in times of need, when our minds are incapable of expressing worship in words of our own. We can become part of the worship of the Universal Church, which we sense is rising to God day after day irrespective of our own situation.

We have noted, however, that by and large our Anglican churches have become captive to middle-class culture. If we are to learn from the past then let it be the persistent failure of the church to reach the working classes of our land that challenges our liturgy. If we seek sound doctrine then our understanding of the church as a 'body of Christ' must cause us to raise the question whether the way that we are using liturgy is not preventing the contributions of different parts of that body. If we seek true worship, then we must allow room not only for valuable tradition but for the real-life feelings, experiences and gifts of our particular congregation.

Flexibility and the ASB
There have indeed been vast improvements in the flexibility of liturgy within the Church of England in the wake of the setting up of a Liturgical Commission in 1955. The period of experimentation which spanned the 1960s and 1970s and resulted in the Alternative Service Book 1980 (ASB) ensures that we will not return to a monochrome liturgy. In the words of the preface to the ASB: 'Rapid social and intellectual changes ... have made it desirable that new understanding of worship should find expression in new forms and styles.' The majority of the Church of England seems to have agreed that flexibility is necessary. That flexibility needs to be used to allow the expression of working-class culture.[1] Our earlier discussions of urban culture and of the nature of worship imply that *at the very least* the maximum use must be made of the freedom allowed for in the ASB.

Sadly, many Anglican churches are still not availing themselves of this freedom. If we consider Evening Prayer: only versicles and responses, a psalm, a reading, a canticle, the Lord's Prayer and a collect are mandatory. These barely fill 20 minutes (or even less!) and it is often

[1] *Faith in the City* Section 6.102.

acknowledged that a suitable hymn, chorus or modern psalm may well replace the canticle. Apart from that, it is hardly twisting the rubrics to make room for various forms of prayer, a sermon or a suitable talk, singing and other contributions to worship. When it comes to services of Holy Communion it is also possible to omit much. The greatest flexibility probably comes in the Intercessions which may be 'led by the president or others' using the set form 'or other suitable words'. At the sharing of the Peace, 'other suitable words' crop up again, and after Communion 'other suitable prayers'. These opportunities are rarely used to their full.

Holy Communion

The Anglican forms of service for Holy Communion are unfortunately the most wordy and the least suited to congregations in Urban Priority Areas. Even the small booklet for Rite A is quite a handful when you are skipping from one section to another. Some congregations have consequently felt that they must provide printed forms of service which are shorter. The Eucharistic Prayers themselves are the chief culprits in respect to wordiness. Carefully fought liturgical and theological battles have left us with monstrously long spoken prayers, often solely the duty of the president. Something of the order of the short Eucharistic Prayer for Use with the Sick is surely called for, if not some prayer shorter still. Freedom is required to leave out or abbreviate more sections on occasions. Many UPA parishes do so already. For example, dare I suggest that the Creed should be optional? The Prayer of Humble Access could be said in its modern form: 'your love compels us to come in' rather than the mind-stretching 'righteousness . . . manifold . . . great mercies . . .'

The increasing presence of children at Parish Communion services provides us with even more impetus for change. At St. Agnes' Burmantofts, where I am currently serving as Curate, once a month the children are all present during the whole Holy Communion service. Their restlessness in the service highlights the need for a more flexible form. We have developed a loose framework for a family service[1], but have not yet felt able radically to alter Rite A Communion to accommodate children. We are currently experimenting with beginning with the welcome, omitting the collect for purity and zipping straight to a rousing song or the sung Gloria (King of Glory setting). You have then reached the Ministry of the Word without much demand on the children to sit still for too long. We then work hard to make the Ministry of the Word more visual (See 4(c) below). A flexible form for *Family* Communion is badly needed, especially if we move towards allowing children to receive communion.

Leadership

If we might assume a flexible structure, who, then, should set the agenda for the week's worship? Ideally the minister would be somebody who had lived, worked and grown up in working-class culture. That is very seldom the case in the Anglican Church at present, and that is at the heart of the

---

[1] Currently: Song—opening prayer/Lord's prayer—one Bible reading—talk—song—(Baptisms)—song—prayers—Offertory hymn—notices—song. Only the Offertory prayer and Lord's prayer are printed, and those are sometimes on O.H.P.

problem. Too often a style of leadership which owes more to middle-class presuppositions than biblical principles or local culture has dominated. If worship is dominated by an articulate, highly-educated white man whose whole upbringing and training has been in an environment quite different from the life-experience of the worshippers whom he leads, there is a very great danger that worship will not reflect the concerns of the local people. Herein lies a block to the mission of the church to working-class culture, and particularly to the inner city. It is as easy for urban dwellers to become dependent on middle-class educated leadership in worship as it is in many other areas of life. If you received a poor education, are unemployed and live in poor housing, the pressures of success and materialism in modern society are likely to leave you with low self-esteem and a feeling of failure or inadequacy. Racism is also a fact of life in our inner cities, and rejection and devaluation are the common experience of many black people. If people are truly to be re-created in worship and drawn up to their full God-given potential, then we must work hard to avoid perpetuating dependence in any way. We must affirm all whom we can by means of real participation in worship. Unfortunately, dependence seems to be a side-effect of some traditional anglo-catholic forms of ministry and worship, with the distinction between the laity and the priest being stressed in many ways. People must not be allowed to be in awe either of the talented individualist, or of the confident speaker, to the extent that they feel that they have nothing to contribute.

Naturally, many inner-city churches will contain people of a wide variety of backgrounds and cultures, even if they are not a 'commuting' church. In these cases each church will need to watch carefully that everybody is being allowed to contribute, and nobody is being excluded even unintentionally. That will be extremely difficult, since at present many churches only survive because of imported middle-class leadership. I am not proposing a new form of inverted snobbery in which all middle-class people are advised to leave inner-city churches, but pointing to the hard questions to be asked of the contribution of the whole body of Christ. Ways must be found for all to give and take from each other in worship.

It is often those churches which have experienced some form of charismatic renewal which have moved furthest in releasing the gifts within the congregation.[1] An acknowledgement of the value of these insights does not necessitate acceptance of any one view of Spirit-baptism or speaking in tongues, but simply belief that the Holy Spirit equips every believer with gifts that can and must be used for the benefit of all. There is to be an inter-dependence amongst the worshippers, and not just a dependence on one or more able leaders. It is salutary to remember that in this century it is the Pentecostal Churches who have often had success in reaching the working-classes.

In order for the worship to be *of* the people, the clergyman must be a facilitator of the people whom he serves—helping them to use their gifts

---

[1] See e.g. Clarry Hendrickse,*One Inner Urban Church and Lay Ministry* (Grove Pastoral Series no. 13, 1983).

and to express their lives in worship. He must, therefore, not be allowed to plan worship alone. Following the lead of such churches as St. Peter's, Everton, we are in the process of setting up a Worship Group. This is to be a working group which considers the content and overall direction of our worship. It will look well ahead at lectionary themes, at Family Services and at 'big' occasions in order to consider where all sorts of contributions—planned or unplanned—should be encouraged. This group arose out of a 'worship review'—an evening to which the whole church was invited, where we 'brainstormed' about the current content of our worship in all its aspects. The group will consist of the vicar, curate, music-group leader/organist, and three lay people, one of whom is deliberately chosen as a mum with small children. With one third of our average congregation of 80-90 being children, this last appointment was thought suitable by the PCC.

Home groups are already responsible for occasional family services (which are held monthly). They can invite one of the clergy to preach if they wish, but the group can plan and lead the whole service. With this sort of contribution being encouraged it is important to note that the clergy actually work *harder,* but more behind the scenes. Some people are able to make contributions at short notice, others will need a lot of advice, encouragement and plenty of time to prepare. The more people are to participate in a service, the more carefully prepared the leader will have to be. With people leading or taking part for the first time there will be mistakes and catastrophes. We have our fair share of embarrassing silences, inaudible readings, and uncertainty over what is happening next. Yet the freedom to make mistakes must be there, as we learn to love and accept each other. We are learning to walk before we run and not to involve *too many* different people 'up front' in one service. The handling of various contributions (especially of the spontaneous in prayer) does not come without failure and discomfort, nor does the discovery of people who can cope with leading a service in such an unpredictable atmosphere.

One strange omission in the worship section of *Faith in the City* is mention of ecumenical services. Elsewhere in the report there are strong pleas that the demands of mission in UPAs necessitate that we work hard on ecumenical partnerships. Joint worship is usually the beginning of this and is also a means of enriching a culture which can be very inward-looking. With the variety of churchmanship within Anglicanism and varieties of culture, there is also much for UPA parishes both to give and to take from other churches in their diocese. Any joint services arranged might well bear in mind these various principles that have been outlined for worship, rather than falling yet again into the trap of clergy-dominated services.

(b) Small is Beautiful
    'Small neighbourhood groupings should join together in worship and other ways as part of the larger Church of the parish'[1]

A further means of encouraging such open contributions in worship is to begin small, in some sort of cell group. Here people can gain the confidence to contribute, here life can be shown to be woven into worship, and here the group or small gathering becomes a natural and

---

[1] *Faith in the City* sections 4.9, 5.45, 6.113 etc.

SOME PRINCIPLES FOR WORSHIP IN UPAs

vital means of support. The worship of the first Christians involved shared lives (Acts 2.42-47). They were one in heart and mind (Acts 4.32) and they shared with those in need among them (4.34). Here was a depth of fellowship which many churches today lack. Our worship services are often devoid of genuine contact. We scarcely know each other at any depth. How can we hope to heal the hurts of our impersonal cities? Christian communities in which the members truly accept one another as Christ accepted them are few and far between. We must seek the help of God's Spirit to engender among us that acceptance and fellowship, which is so central to the gospel, and give the Spirit a chance by starting small.

If an individual is to make an open contribution to worship he will need to trust the other worshippers. This will be particularly true of requests for prayer on personal matters, and of tentative offering of gifts of one sort or another. A degree of openness and trust is required—an atmosphere in which people are free to fail, or admit their failings without fear of ridicule. This will not come easily to large congregations, if at all. The problem is exaggerated in UPAs since many of the disadvantaged people in our cities experience a lethargy and a lack of self-confidence which result in them sitting passively to receive. They need a small and accepting group.

Since working-class community is more group-based and less individualistic, the informal home group based on streets or areas could be an invaluable growth area in which both gifts are discovered and new disciples made. Worshipping in a home also demonstrates the involvement of God in the nitty-gritty of people's lives, the non-separation of Jesus and the community in which people live. Such groups may also be formed of people who would not be ready to go to church and join the full eucharistic community. Small natural groupings may have the effect of producing a truly working-class untraditionalist Christianity.

It must be remembered, however, that the meeting places in working-class culture are not usually each other's homes, but places such as the pub, working men's club, and bingo hall. It is also noticeable that men and women will more often socialize separately. The emphasis is perhaps on going out to *do* something with a group of people. The attractiveness of house groups may therefore not be so much that 'we come to *be* together every week' but that 'we come together to *do* this once a week for three weeks', for example, a Lent course of prayer, or a series of videos. The focus and the task of each meeting will need to be crystal clear. The expectation of a weekly talking shop is a real turn-off, especially at the start of a group. The desire for fellowship, being together, is something that grows.

The importance of the 'house group' is certainly a recurring theme in many growing churches in UPAs. Such structures are now prevalent, of course, in many suburban churches. Yet the need to move away from an individual view of spirituality makes the issue even more pressing in churches in UPAs. Many Christians have been taught that their individual *private* devotions are the key to success in their walk with God. It is undeniable that such devotions are a great source of strength for many—and I include myself. Yet we must ask if this is simply middle-class individualism raising its head again. It may often be that people do not live in a situation which allows them to find either the time or the place alone to have the traditional evangelical 'quiet time'. It is not that such practices are unhelpful, but that people who are used to strongly corporate activities must not be led to feel that they are failing if they do not pray and study their Bible alone daily. An over-emphasis on learning God's will intellectually from a book (the Bible) on your own can simply increase the sense of powerlessness which some people feel. This will particularly affect those who are not at home with books (perhaps even being illiterate or sub-literate) and those who are happier with group-based activity. The answer to this may be to promote both group-based reading of the Bible, and group prayer.

The small group, then, can be an area where the true nature of Christianity is worked out, with all its radical demands on relationships. It can also be a less alienating environment in which those more used to group-based activity can find the presence of God. We must beware of promoting a one-sided spirituality which focuses on individuals being 'fed' by God rather than people expressing the nature of God in the world in which they live. As Neville Black expressed it:

> 'The inner city may . . . have much to teach the church about new resources of the spiritual in the world at large: new dynamics of spirituality in which the corporate is strong, and . . . activity, action and demonstration are as important as the personal and the pietistic.'[1]

That sort of living, putting ourselves on the line in interacting with both believers and non-believers, needs all the power that God's spirit can give, and all the support our brothers and sisters in Christ can give.

(c) Promoting the Visual

> Communicating 'through feeling rather than the mind, through non-verbal rather than verbal'.[2]

The earlier discussion on forms of communication in working-class culture will hopefully have shown that we should be seriously considering the complementation of the verbal by the visual in our UPA worship. The concrete and the tangle should outweigh the abstract and the theoretical.[3] This should serve to assist people in our Urban Priority Area churches to grasp more easily what faith and worship is about, and to feel able to contribute, since the visual expressions of worship would be more natural to them.

It is in the area of the visual and the symbolic that anglo-catholicism has had much to contribute. Sixteenth century protestantism, in reaction against many abuses of sacrament and symbol, emphasized the importance of God's written word, stripping away much colourful mythology and symbolism. As necessary as this may have been at the time, it is clear that words alone cannot express the mystery of God. Could it be that restricting God's grace largely to a book of words has closed channels of communication with God for those who are strangers to books and reading?

There will be a mystery about some of our worship which will be expressed in symbolism which is timeless. We must not expect everyone who enters a church immediately to understand all the imagery which

---
[1] Neville Black *Spirituality of the City,* Tape from *Greenbelt* Festival (ICC Studios, 1983).
[2] *Faith in the City* section 6:114.
[3] *Faith in the City* section 6:104.

SOME PRINCIPLES FOR WORSHIP IN UPAs

confronts them. God is not immediately understood by the human mind. We should not totally succumb to the sort of rationalist and scientific thinking which would remove all mythology from our society. There is still scope to help people to 'imagine their way through the gate of heaven'.[1] Symbols are not *so* strange to modern man. our life is littered with outward signs which convey an inner meaning—from lighting the Olympic flame to cutting a wedding cake. Let us explore symbolism.

Lent, Holy Week and Easter in particular provide us with great scope for expressing our worship in visual terms: the Imposition of Ashes on Ash Wednesday was found to be a very moving service by many when used as an experiment here; the stripping of the church and the uncovering of a crucifix on Maundy Thursday or Good Friday; the Service of Light on Easter Day.[2] Light is also a powerful symbol of Christmas, especially at Christingle and in the lighting of an Advent Wreath. The wreath has been used here at St. Agnes with great effect, the children thoroughly involved as week by week more of them were involved in its lighting.

In the use of all such ceremonies the symbolism should be accessible and not obscure. Some ancient symbolism will need explaining, but will thereby provide a visual teaching aid. Yet alongside the timeless symbolism of water, bread and wine, oil, light and darkness there should be room for the discovery of symbols which rise up from the common experience of the worshippers. Here is room for use of the images portrayed by the artists of our time, be they pop singers, poets, painters, or dancers. The gospel and the world must be allowed to interact. There is room for the traditional and there is room for the modern, flowing from the life-experiences of the worshippers.[3] Neither should the traditional liturgical calendar be despised. The ceremony and colour associated with the lectionary gives a shape and sense of movement in the passing of the seasons which is of great value in the monotonous greyness of many urban people's experience. Here is a rhythm of life for those who have lost the rhythm of employed life.

It might therefore appear that there is truth in the claim that the 'high' churchmen have discovered expressions of worship which are particularly suited to the cultures we have described. Yet there are many consequences of traditional anglo-catholic worship and doctrine which appear positively unhelpful in the light of the preceeding discussion. The dominance of the priest, set apart from the worshippers, can encourage a sense of dependence which serves to inhibit just the sense of participation which needs encouraging. The feeling that God is on our side intimately involved and interested in our doings must not be submerged by elaborate ritual which removes God to the far distance. While the actual physical participation of the worshippers in ceremonies and the gestures is powerful in its way, it is no substitute for sharing experiences of life, for shared leadership of worship, or shared planning of worship.

[1] Killinger *Leave it to the Spirit* (SCM, 1971)—see chapters 6-8.
[2] The *Lent, Holy Week and Easter* Services published in 1986 are rich in these and other visual possibilities, including the Passion Narratives in Dramatic Form, and even a foot-washing ceremony for the adventurous! (Church House Publishing).
[3] See Michael Marshall *Renewal in Worship* (Marshalls, 1982) and Killinger (*op. cit.*) for explorations of relevant modern symbolism.

WORSHIP IN THE CITY

Let us all also ponder the suggestion that a single *man*, dressed in fine robes (or wearing an academic hood), standing between the people and the holy table, is giving off signals that training and education stand between the ordinary person and God? But, in truth it is not the priest alone who has a close relationship with God. There is nothing that he has done which makes him more acceptable to God than the other worshippers. Naturally, in large church buildings with many worshippers it may be suitable for the minister to be distinguished from the congregation. Many church buildings do force an unsuitable position for the minister upon us, but it does not always have to be so. At the very least the holy table can often be brought closer to the people, and the priest positioned behind it. In some buildings it will be possible to worship 'around' the holy table in some way. That sort of symbolism, expressing the universal priesthood of all present, should be our aim.

Since the gospel we proclaim is of a kingdom which applies to man in all his doings, in every aspect of his personality, it is suitable to address man via all his senses. The imagination as well as the intellect needs to be given its place in worship. Music, colour and silence all play their part in this. There can be the acting of a biblical story, or short dramas. The musician, artist, dancer, the singer, and the flower arranger can bring their gifts to worship God. This should not be the province of the 'arty'. The Sunday School should be encouraged to bring into church its drawings and other work. Simplicity, and forms of expression which are natural to the congregation are the important criteria, not artistic excellence or perfection (other than giving of your best to God). The range of backgrounds represented in an inner-city church can provide a rich mosaic of colourful talent which can glorify God—from a Betjeman poem to a folk guitar to a West Indian gospel song. The gifts are there to be discovered, perhaps in small informal settings first: for example the harvest supper, carol singing or a service at an Old Folks home. Worship may also tend to be characterized by more informal active involvement—clapping, hugging at the peace, raised hands, crossing oneself (all of which, incidentally, may become formalities and lose their meaning).

The preacher must bear in mind the importance of the visual in his sermons, evoking the imagination in many different ways, and leaving people with pictorial images which express the heart of what he has said. Here the overhead projector, the slide/tape presentation and the video screen will figure regularly. The preaching will not always be a lecture, but more informal, telling stories, using mimicry, encouraging dialogue—an all-round experience. At St. Agnes we have recently experimented with six videos[1] during the evening service. The format was: abbreviated Evening Prayer, 15 minute video, a break for a song, a second 15 minutes of video, discussion and then different forms of prayer and/or a song to finish with.

The atmosphere of the building is also very important—beauty and colour which speak of the attractiveness and welcome of God, banners, pictures, flowers and displays. And warm and comfortable—like a pub or a home! Our God is neither cold nor austere. The emotional atmosphere of worship will speak more powerfully than words (Three cheers for the charismatic movement!).

---

[1] *Jesus Then and Now* (Lella) Not bad, but we await such teaching videos which are even more snappy in their format, changing pace and content every few minutes, with less talking heads.

SOME PRINCIPLES FOR WORSHIP IN UPAs

As we seek visible and tangible demonstrations of the kingdom of God to communities to whom God is largely irrelevant, I suggest that the ministry of healing has an important part to play. Crowds of ordinary people flocked to Jesus not only because of his sparkling preaching with its visual images from everyday life, but because they could *see* the kingdom demonstrated in healings in front of their eyes. John Wimber and his team attracted interest not only in suburban charismatic Bible-belts, but also in Christian communities in inner urban areas.

I say this tentatively, since there is some work to be done in clarifying and integrating the two polarized 'kingdom' theologies currently doing the rounds, one seeing charismatic signs and wonders as the signs of the kingdom, the other seeking social justice. It is sometimes asserted that charismatic styles of ministry only develop in the introverted luxury of middle-class suburbia. This would seem to have some truth in it, partly, because charismatics have shied away from the social involvement which becomes part and parcel of UPA church life, and partly because the lack of self-confidence evident in UPAs hinders the free expression of 'personal' gifts. Yet it is my conviction and experience that God does heal, and it is almost incidental that this is a tangible sign of his presence to people who do not want *arguments* but *action*. With us, people who have received communion may move through into a quiet side chapel for the laying on of hands by church leaders (lay and ordained).

(d) Bringing in Life

The Church will 'gather up and inform local life'[1]

Both our definition of worship as the dedication of our whole lives to God and the tendency of working-class speech patterns to communicate in terms of the real and actual, would suggest that we must attempt to express the wholeness of life in our worship. In prayers, preaching and story the variety of experiences and feelings of the worshippers and of the local community must be brought into public worship to demonstrate the redemption of all life by God: 'the importance of the ordinary'.[2]

In prayer, huge and general 'blanket prayers' should often give way to the specific. The local community should figure highly,[3] acknowledging the joys and problems of every sort of person in the area, from one-parent families to teachers, from children to senior citizens. In St. Agnes there have been prayers for the dangerous structure of a local school and worried parents; for a campaign to get a pelican crossing on a busy road; for those affected by water-supply problems. Neither has the prayer been divorced from practical action in each case (to the extent of blocking the entire Urban Motorway by means of a local demonstration!). The world of work and everyday life will enter in.[4] Flickers of hope, signs of God's presence, can be celebrated—self-sacrifice, breaking down of barriers of prejudice, fair officials, generosity, resilience under pressure, those who help the handicapped or elderly. Looking for signs of the advancing kingdom rather than dwelling solely on the problems will be a source of encouragement, opening people's eyes to the presence of God and the possibilities of fulness of life. Here is the tension referred to earlier—the acknowledgement of the real problems and sorrows of life, but also the celebration of the kingdom of God among us and advancing.

[1] *Faith in the City* section 6:102.   [2] *Faith in the City* section 6:109.   [3] *ibid* 6:100.
[4] Butland *Work in Worship* (Hodder 1985) is a useful anthology of readings and prayers.

WORSHIP IN THE CITY

Yet perhaps the greater danger in the city is that we do not bring the world into our worship. The structures must be free enough to allow expression of the lives of the worshippers. There will be a place for 'story' or 'testimony'[2]—'tell us how you got on at the hospital this week', 'who wants to tell us about something good that they praised God for this week?', 'did God answer your prayers of last week?' If the worshippers have been offering acceptable worship to God all week through caring, through working for justice and through loving service, there will be stories to be told. Stories that will encourage and stories that will lead to prayer. Community festivals, school events, sporting achievements, local elections, political issues, will all find their places in notices, prayers and noticeboard displays. At several inner-city churches I know everybody gives his or her own notices—if carefully 'chaired' that too can add to the sense of worth and belonging.

The content of preaching will also be affected. It will be rich in its application to life. It should not rely so often on the linear development of concepts and ideas, but on the concrete and everyday. It may well learn from the insights of Liberation Theology, and build *from* life examples *to* biblical concepts, and not *vice versa*. For example, since indigenous forms of speech also follow that inductive direction of thought (that is, from the specific to the general), then communication may be facilitated. It almost goes without saying that the ordained educated man will not be the only preacher. If the culture is rich in story-telling then let the stories be told, and *maybe* the minister will draw out a few conclusions from the stories if that helps further.

Several ministers who have moved from suburban churches to the inner-city mentioned to me the switch in emphasis in their preaching towards acceptance and hope. In UPAs many people are without hope, unstable in relationships, disadvantaged in education, income and housing. Such people need encouragement, belief in a God who can effect change, a certainty amongst the uncertainties. Images of Jesus as friend may predominate over images of Jesus as king, judge or ruler. To caricature the situation: a middle-class congregation may require their pride and stability undermined by an emphasis on God's judgment, an inner-city congregation may require assurance of their worth before God.

(e) Making music
There are some questions that we must ask ourselves about the musical side of our worship in UPAs, even if the answers are not immediately clear. There is a tendency to limit the debate about church music to 'ancient versus modern' or 'hymns versus choruses' but I would suggest that there are deeper issues.

There is some truth in the assertion that unchurched people from non-book cultures 'do not readily read the prose-type, five-verse Wesley and Watts songs of yesteryear, but can and do remember simple, Bible-based songs or choruses'.[2] One of the most meaningful worship songs I ever

[1] *Faith in the City* section 6.104.
[2] Dave Cave *What is Worship* in *'City Cries'* No. 5 Summer 1984. This thematic issue of the Journal of the Evangelical Urban Training Project is on 'worship in the urban context'.

SOME PRINCIPLES FOR WORSHIP IN UPAs

hears was incredibly simple in its content, written and bashed out on a cheap guitar by a Merseyside lad and the rest of the youth group. It was *their* song, their giving of worth to God, yet they still had something to gain from more ancient expressions of the majesty of God. There is room for both: the traditional and tested with their depth of imagery and poetry; and immediacy and accessibility of simple choruses. Neither, of course, are we without modern hymns of depth.

The fact that men are hugely reticent to sing (in church, that is, not on the terraces or in the pub!) is more noticeable in UPAs. There are two factors which may explain this. Firstly, the honesty already referred to will discourage lads from singing unless they have a real conviction about the subject-matter of the song (e.g. West Ham being the greatest football team in the world).[1] Secondly, the 'taboo on tenderness'[2] which can be seen in urban society. Many of the men have been brought up in a tough street world where aggression was the only means of survival. Those who work, operate in a hard, competitive world. The macho man-of-the-streets image that many men try to live up to is not served by attending supposedly 'wet' church services. Similarly, for many urban teenagers it is the aggressive driving force of punk rock, heavy metal and electro-funk that best express their feelings. (Or at least, it suits the hard exterior that they cultivate in order to survive in a society that shows little sign of caring about them.) Whilst there is clearly something in this aggressiveness which needs redeeming, and an inevitable tenderness in some of our relationship with our heavenly father that the Spirit will cultivate in the hardest man, I simply warn of the effect of following the tendency in some renewal circles to sing mostly repetitive and sloppy love songs to Jesus. Do we not mis-represent our God if we *only* portray sentimentality in our worship? I wonder if many of the songs of the renewal movement would be different if they had not been written in comfortable suburbia? Many are entirely concerned with the wonders of the heavenly realm, at the expense of connecting with the harshness of urban life. I know that a vision of the risen Christ and his ultimate victory is necessary, but the 'praise-the-Lord-anyway' mentality is not a universal remedy for pain and suffering. Once more the range of moods expressed in the Psalms is a precedent for us. Our greatest danger of over-balance at the present time is towards a diet of songs entirely about victory. In the end this does not satisfy—it is in danger of increasing the sense of failure among the worshippers, because 'I don't see Jesus in control here like that'.

At St. Agnes therefore, we work extremely hard to choose music which is true to our situation, but also that which lifts us out of it in praise of Christ.[3] Neither the vicar nor the organist/music group leader should be allowed to choose all the music themselves, and the simple bible-based choruses will come into their own in more 'open' worship, such as during the administration of communion or (for us) the informality of the prayer times in the smaller evening services. An extremely popular evening series adopted a 'Songs of Praise' style. Each week a church member or a married couple would use their favourite hymns as a framework for the service, and explain why each was important to them.

---

[1] The only undisputable fact in this booklet.
[2] Thompson, *op. cit.*
[3] We use *Cry Hosanna*. We also duplicate—but find copyright costs prohibitive.

WORSHIP IN THE CITY

The careful professionalism of much church music must take second place if the informality and spontaneity of UPA culture is to emerge. We will still work hard, and give God of our *best* in music, Yet it must be the best and most natural expression of the talents of *all* the congregation, and not just one virtuoso organist (who is frequently 'imported' anyway). At St. Agnes, the formal choir (and its choir pews!) has been replaced by a music group of mixed age and ability, accompanied by a mixture of organ, piano and guitar. The last song of each morning service is a great cacophony of sound, as children come out to the front and grab a tambourine, cymbal or other percussion instrument from a box and join in. If the church is drawing worshippers from a multi-racial community, then it is almost inevitable that there will be rich musical backgrounds to draw upon as well.

(f) Learning about Silence

Silence is said to be a difficult thing for worshippers in UPAs to cope with. The city is a place of great noise and bustle. Homes have a constant background of noise—radio, music, television. Silence can therefore be a very threatening experience to some. Huge cold and silent churches are not as helpful and 'numinous' in quality to some as we might think. Some will find it more relaxing to enter a church where there is constant chatter and a physically warm welcome—and children!

Yet every culture benefits from being sufficiently outward-looking to learn from others, and the church especially is to be cross-cultural, breaking down the barriers of race, class and sex (Gal.3.28). By careful usage, silence can become a valuable tool in Urban Spirituality. There is to be found in silence a release from prayers that rely on words, and a release of all our senses to imagine the presence of God.

> 'Rather than suggest that silence . . . is an alien experience . . . best left out of worship . . . we ought to offer the experience in ways that will catch people's imagination, give them a taste of a new dimension and gently lead them further into the mystery of God.'[1]

In time that silence which is the presence of the Holy Spirit, comes.

If silence is to be longer than ten or fifteen seconds then it should be directed in some way. It could be for private prayer; for reflection on an attribute of God; for meditation on a biblical story or verse, a saying, somebody's story, a picture or series of slides; for guided meditation (perhaps imagining yourself as one of the characters in a Bible story); or simply to be still and to be aware of the presence of God. Silence in the small group may be the first step. Some may be troubled by it, but others who will find a great release in it. Its use is a matter of freedom:

> 'freedom to employ both sound and silence as building blocks, as ingredients in an experience we are fashioning, partly consciously and partly as a happening which goes beyond our control'.[2]

Our images of God can be bound by words. Let God himself make nonsense of our speech and transcend our small images of him.

The ASB allows for silence in many places, e.g. prior to confession, during the intercessions, before and after communion. Listening to God within that silence, people can be encouraged to share a Bible verse or a mental 'picture' that they believe God has given them, or a tongue or prophecy.

[1] David Emmott, Letter to *City Cries* No. 6 Autumn 1984 in response to Issue No. 5.
[2] Killinger *op. cit.*, p.135.

5. SUMMARY: LESSONS FOR THE WIDER CHURCH

The urgency of the church's mission in UPAs has caused us to ask questions about the fulness of the expression of Christianity in such areas and has also led us in search of cultural expessions of worship. It has been noted that the root of the problem is the gap between the middle-classness of the established churches and the predominantly working-class UPA population.

It seems clear that worship must be allowed to breathe life, because our true worship is our whole lives. We must be assisted to bring all we are to worship, to share with the community who are working for and looking for the kingdom, and celebrating its coming. This demands of the Church of England especially a relaxing of its hold on worship from the top and the allowing of a true meeting of the congregation. The larger 'celebration' of scores of people on Sundays will need to be complemented and fed by the close fellowship of small groups.

Our understanding of communication in working-class cultures demands that our worship be more colourful, pictorial and experience-based. Both this observation, and the multi-ethnic nature of many UPAs, necessitates a letting-go of the control of worship by middle-class leadership to allow the truly local people to speak and communicate with God and each other in their own way. This will probably result in more group-based tasks, and less individualism.

These questions at their simplest can be addressed to the wider church—are the wide concerns of the kingdom of God, sacred and secular, individual and corporate, adequately expressed in our services of worship? Once more, the questions confronting us in Urban Priority Areas are really a distillation or a sharpening-up of the questions which face the whole church of God in England.

Worship and life are inextricably bound together. Family relationships, poverty, social security benefits, the Arms Race, racism . . . none of these issues is 'off limits' for our God; we bring all that we are, all our concerns, into worship. Neither our Christianity nor our worship is to be escapist. It may also be that, in a society where the power of the printed words is fast being overtaken by the impact of the video screen and the advertising hoarding, the return to more visual means of communication also has much to teach the whole church. UPAs are not the only 'non-book cultures' in which we people of The Book of Life have to communicate our faith.

APPENDIX 1: SELECT BIBLIOGRAPHY

John Benington *Culture, Class and Christian Beliefs* (Scripture Union, 1973)
Raimundo Panikkar *Worship and Secular Man* (DLT, 1973)
Bruce Reed *The Dynamics of Religion* (DLT, 1978)
Paul Walker *The Church and the Working Class* (Unpublished Dissertation, St. John's College, Nottingham, 1984)
There are also Grove Booklets in the Ethics and Pastoral Series, responding to *Faith in the City*—Ethics no. 61, *Hope in the City,* edited by Greg Forster, and Pastoral no. 26, *On from Faith in the City* edited by David Newman—forming a threesome with this Booklet.

APPENDIX 2: SECTION ON WORSHIP FROM *FAITH IN THE CITY*

Worship

6.99 At the heart of our vision, as it has emerged over the last two years, is a commitment to God and his call, and the faithful response of his Church in the UPAs. We believe that such a Church will be locally-rooted and outward-looking, and that its worship will properly reflect this.

6.100 For the local UPA Church to respond to God by commending his gospel, it must talk people's language, so that they have a chance of hearing and understanding. What is sometimes called the 'incarnational' side of the Christian religion is an indispensable characteristic of a worshipping community. The Church in the UPA has to live in and be part of the local world. The roots of liturgy must be found in the ground of society.

6.101 Worship in the UPAs must emerge out of and reflect local cultures: it will always be the worship of him who is totally Other and yet is to be found, worshipped and served through the realities of UPA life. The worship of the Church that is part of the UPA will be the worship of a Church that is present in celebration, confession, compassion and judgment.

6.102 To understand worship in this way means that certain aspects of UPA life will necessarily greatly affect the formation of the worshipping life of the UPA Church. The main contribution of the Church to our cities is to be itself, and true to its vocation. It will gather up and inform local life. It must 'accept the positive aspects and validity of working class culture, particularly to build on the strong sense of family and community which is often found, and be prepared to communicate through feeling rather than the mind, through non-verbal communication rather than verbal'.* It will be more informal and flexible in its use of urban language, vocabulary, style and content. It will therefore reflect a universality of form with local variations, allowing significant space for worship which is genuinely local, expressed in and through local cultures, and reflecting the local context.

6.103 It will promote a greater *involvement* of the congregations in worship. Some clergy and lay people seem to have the idea that anyone with a Cockney or West Indian accent could not possibly read a lesson or lead the intercessions. Their voices may therefore never be heard throughout the service in the heart of the East End of London, Toxteth or Moss Side.

6.104 It will reflect the concern of local UPA people for things to be more concrete and tangible rather than abstract and theoretical. This finds expression in the use of religious objects like banners designed and made locally, as well as more traditional symbols like crucifixes. Worship and study may therefore lay more emphasis on the history, the story, the narrative. Local UPA people often love to tell the stories of their lives, how God changed them, of problems overcome, and of great events and disasters.

6.105 People should be encouraged to come and go—to come into Church when they want to or need to. Many Churches convey an attitude

---

* Submission from the Diocese of Birmingham.

APPENDIX

of spirituality which makes prayer and worship available only to those who turn up in the right place at the right time and go through the correct motions corporately from start to finish.

6.106 The worship offered by the local Churches is also important as a means of evangelism. The stranger who comes into services will make a judgment about Christianity on the basis of what he encounters there. Is the worship lively and participatory? Does it evoke a sense of the presence of God while showing a concern for the real things in people's lives? Much of this will depend on how the local congregation order their services.

6.107 Worship is about good dreams: it needs to hold them alongside what is sometimes a very harsh reality. UPA Christians want a beautiful service, but they may have to go home to domestic violence or a leaking roof. A Church life which has nothing to say about these things simply leaves people feeling inferior. They feel they must hide from the clergy and the local Church their debts, their court cases, their sufferings at the hands of their husbands. Reality must be faced. There must be something to understand about God's will for a wife terrified of her husband, for a husband terrified of his gambling debts, for parents who dread that their son is out beating up Bangladeshis.

6.108 Worship will put the harsh realities in a new light. It may enable people to withdraw for a time from the pressures, but it will be 'withdrawal with intent to return', not evasion.

6.109 Running through all the aspects of UPA life as they need to affect worship is the firm and hopeful recognition of 'the importance of the ordinary'. It is that which is so often missing from Church life and witness in UPAs. It can only be properly accepted by a truly local Church.

6.110 Many submissions included suggestions about books, services and groups. As we noted in Chapter 3 to give people a 1300 page Alternative Service Book is a symptom of the gulf between the Church and ordinary people in the UPAs. We have heard calls for short, functional service booklets or cards, prepared by people who will always ask 'if all the words are really necessary'. The work of reforming the liturgy has really only just begun for the UPA Church, and we *recommend* that the Liturgical Commission pays close attention to the needs of Churches in the UPAs.

6.111 There has also been a clear plea that the formal liturgies so beloved of the wider Church must be complemented in UPAs by more informal and spontaneous acts of worship and witness. Vivid and concrete manifestations of spirituality have proven track records in many UPAs—like, for example, the Way of the Cross acted out through the streets of the East End, Armley, Euston, Notting Hill, Cardiff and Bradford.

6.112 Worship which encourages informality and spontaneity will not dispense with care and preparation. The local UPA Church wil be as concerned with the beauty of worship and its excellence as are often the local schools with their productions.

6.113 We have already affirmed the importance of small groups in the local Church, in its mission and in its worship. Yet they need to be complemented by the glorious occasions and celebrations in the local parish Church.

STOCK LIST—GROVE BOOKLETS ON MINISTRY & WORSHIP [Nos. 1-70]
and GROVE WORSHIP SERIES [71 onwards]

The Worship Series (of 24 pages each) is now published four times a year. All titles cost **90p**. Numbers not included below are out of print. Asterisked titles are in a second edition or reprint.

- *12. **The Language of Series 3** by David L. Frost
- *13. **What Priesthood has the Ministry?** by J. M. R. Tillard
- *14. **Recent Liturgical Revision in the Church of England** by Colin Buchanan (**£1.70**) †
- 14A. **Supplement for 1973-4 to Recent Liturgical Revision in the Church of England** by Colin Buchanan
- 14B. **Supplement for 1974-6 to Recent Liturgical Revision in the Church of England** by Colin Buchanan
- 14C. **Supplement for 1976-8 to Recent Liturgical Revision in the Church of England** by Colin Buchanan
- 14D. See Liturgical Study 39 (**£1.70**) †
- 15. **Institutions and Inductions** by Trevor Lloyd
- 16. **Alternative Eucharistic Prayers** by Derek Billings
- *20. **A Case for Infant Baptism** by Colin Buchanan
- *24. **Infant Baptism under Cross-Examination** by David Pawson and Colin Buchanan
- 29. **The Ordinal and its Revision** by Peter Toon
- 30. **Liturgy and Creation** by Peter R. Akehurst
- 32. **Inaugural Services** Edited by Colin Buchanan
- 34. **Modern Roman Catholic Worship: The Mass** by Nicholas Sagovsky
- *35. **Drama in Worship** by Andy Kelso
- 40. **Freedom in a Framework: Some Possibilities with Series 3** by Richard More
- *42. **Christian Healing in the Parish** by Michael Botting
- 43. **Modern Roman Catholic Worship: Baptism and Penance** by Nicholas Sagovsky
- *44. **Exorcism, Deliverance and Healing: Some Pastoral Guidelines** by John Richards
- 50. **Evangelicals, Obedience and Change** by Trevor Lloyd
- 52. **Inter-Faith Worship?** by Peter Akehurst and Dick Wootton
- 53. **Penance** by David Gregg
- *55. **Urban Church Growth: Some Clues from Britain and South America** by Eddie Gibbs
- 60. **Liturgy for Ordination: The Series 3 Services** by Michael Sansom
- *61. **One Baptism Once** by Colin Buchanan
- *62. **Preaching at Funerals** by Ian Bunting
- *64. **Grow Through Groups** by Eddie Gibbs
- 65. **Liturgy for Initiation: The Series 3 Services** by Colin Buchanan
- 66. **Encountering Westindian Pentecnstalism: its Ministry and Worship** by John Root
- 67. **How Do Congregations Learn?** by David Gillett
- 68. **Liturgy for Communion: The Revised Series 3 Service** by Colin Buchanan
- 69. **The Attractive Church** by Kenneth White
- *70. **Preaching at Baptisms** by Gordon Ogilvie
- 71. **A Hymn Book Survey 1962-1980** by Robin A. Leaver
- 72. **A Late-Night Service: Compline in Modern English** by Mark Davies (also an offprint of the service)
- 73. **Family Festivals: An Approach to Worship in the Home** compiled by Michael Vasey, Tom Jamieson, Lyn Jamieson, Dan Young and Sue Young
- *74. **Preaching at Weddings** by Ian Bunting
- 75. **Ceremonial in Worship** by Trevor Lloyd
- 76. **Leading Worship** by Colin Buchanan
- 77. **Intercessions in Worship** by Michael Vasey
- 78. **Preaching at Communion (i)** by Ian Bunting
- 79. **Preaching at Communion (ii)** by Ian Bunting
- 80. **The Kiss of Peace** by Colin Buchanan
- 81. **Hymns in Today's Language?** by Chris Idle
- 82. **Eucharistic Concelebration** by John Fenwick
- 83. **Renewing the Congregation's Music** by David Parkes
- 84. **Liturgy for the Sick: The New Church of England Services** by Colin Buchanan and David Wheaton
- 85. **Welcoming Children to Communion** by Dan Young
- 86. **ARCIC and Lima on Baptism and Eucharist** by Colin Buchanan
- 87. **Introducing Liturgical Change** by Trevor Lloyd
- 88. **Welcoming the Bishop** by David Cutts
- 89. **Preaching on Special Occasions** by Charles Hutchins
- 90. **Evangelical Anglicans and Liturgy** by Colin Buchanan
- 91. **Adult Baptisms** by Colin Buchanan
- 92. **Evangelical Anglicans and the Lima Text** by Tony Price
- 93. **Celebrating Lent Holy Week and Easter** by Trevor Lloyd
- 94. **Reading the Bible at the Eucharist** by Michael Vasey
- 95. **Worship in the Inner City** by John Bentham

ISSN 0144–1728   **ISBN** 1 85174 024 4

GROVE BOOKS LIMITED
BRAMCOTE   NOTTS.   NG9 3DS (0602-251114)

Printed by Hassall & Lucking Ltd., Cross Street, Long Eaton, Nottingham NG10 1HD   Tel. L.E. 733292